Contents

What is a humanitarian organisation?   4

About Save the Children   5

History of Save the Children   6

The founders of Save the Children   8

Early work   9

Core values of Save the Children   10

How Save the Children works   11

Where in the world is Save the Children?   12

Timeline   13

Concerns, campaigns and classic actions   14

     Inadequate health care   14

     Inadequate education   16

     Lack of children's rights   18

     Lack of emergency protection   20

The people of Save the Children   22

   WORKNESH MEKONNEN   Director of fundraising and sponsorship   22

   GARY SHAYE   Field office director   24

   FIONA FARLEY   Project manager, education   26

   ADAM KEEHN   Field office director   28

What can you do?   30

Glossary   31

Index   32

Glossary words

When a word is printed in **bold**, its meaning is included on that page. You can also look up its meaning in the Glossary on page 31.

What is a humanitarian organisation?

Humanitarian organisations work to help solve problems in countries around the world, wherever there is a need for their help. They are sometimes called aid agencies, not-for-profit or non-government organisations (NGOs). Some organisations, such as Greenpeace, work to protect the environment. Others, such as Amnesty International and the International Red Cross, work to protect people's **human rights** or provide for their basic needs in times of conflict and disaster. Doctors Without Borders sends **volunteers** anywhere in the world to give medical help to people affected by disasters. Groups like Save the Children and Australian Volunteers International help rebuild communities that need food, education and advice.

Some humanitarian organisations are given money by governments to help run their programs. They also work hard to collect enough money from the public to keep going. Some of their workers are volunteers and are not paid, while others work for a small wage.

The *Humanitarian Organisations* series focusses on six well-known organisations and explains how they help those in need around the world.

Australian Volunteers International

The Red Cross

Greenpeace

Save the Children

Amnesty International

Doctors Without Borders

Humanitarian Organisations

Save the Children

Ann Parry

MACMILLAN
LIBRARY

For Jack and Win Parry—exceptional and loving parents.

First published in 2005 by
MACMILLAN EDUCATION AUSTRALIA PTY LTD
627 Chapel Street, South Yarra 3141

Visit our website at www.macmillan.com.au

Associated companies and representatives throughout the world.

National Library of Australia
Cataloguing-in-Publication data

Parry, Ann, 1949–.
    Save the children.

    Includes index.
    For upper primary school students.
    ISBN 0 7329 9742 9.

    1. Save the Children Fund – Juvenile literature. I. Title.
    (Series: Parry, Ann, 1949– Humanitarian organisations).

362.7

Edited by Angelique Campbell-Muir and Anna Fern
Cover and text design by Raul Diche
Maps by Pat Kermode
Photo research by Legend Images

Printed in China

Acknowledgements
The author and the publisher are grateful to the following for permission to reproduce copyright material:

Cover photographs: Save the Children feeding centre in Ethiopia, courtesy of Save the Children/Michael Bisceglie.
Students in Iraq, courtesy of Save the Children US. Students in classroom, courtesy of Save the Children.

Amnesty International, p. 4 (logo); Australian Red Cross, p. 4 (logo); Australian Volunteers International, p. 4 (logo);
Doctors Without Borders/Médecins Sans Frontières (MSF), p. 4 (logo); Greenpeace, p. 4 (logo); Save the Children, pp. 1, 4
(logo), 5, 8, 10, 11, 14, 16, 17, 18, 21, 22, 23, 26, 27, 28, 30; Save the Children Bolivia, pp. 24, 25; Save the Children UK, pp. 6, 7,
9, 19; Save the Children US, p. 15; Save the Children/Michael Bisceglie, pp. 20, 29.

While every care has been taken to trace and acknowledge copyright, the publisher tenders their apologies for any
accidental infringement where copyright has proved untraceable. Where the attempt has been unsuccessful, the
publisher welcomes information that would redress the situation.

Please note
At the time of printing, the Internet addresses appearing in this book were correct. Owing to the dynamic nature of the
Internet, however, we cannot guarantee that all these addresses will remain correct.

About Save the Children

Save the Children is an international relief and development organisation. It began in the United Kingdom in 1919. Now it operates in more than 100 countries around the world, helping millions of people in thousands of communities. Its work is based around the rights of children. These rights are now listed in the **United Nations Convention** on the Rights of the Child.

Working with communities

Save the Children works with communities to help them sort out and understand the problems they are facing, and find solutions. They also find ways to help children achieve a better future. Their main aim is to give children the opportunity to lead safe and healthy lives, by giving them the special care they need.

Save the Children uses various methods to do this, but always tries to work with communities so that they can become more self-sufficient, supplying their own needs, such as food, water and shelter.

Did you know?

The year 1999 marked the 80th anniversary of Save the Children and the 10th anniversary of the United Nations Convention on the Rights of the Child.

Glossary word

United Nations Convention
a treaty or legal agreement, for example, about children's rights, signed by the member countries of the UN

Save the Children

This is the logo for the Save the Children Fund.

History of Save the Children

When World War I finally ended in 1918, the Allied Forces (which included England, France, Canada and Australia) had convinced their enemies (which included Germany and Austria) to sign a peace treaty. One of the reasons these countries gave in was that a blockade had been set up to prevent food, medicine and other goods from reaching them. This had a serious effect, particularly on the children. Many died of starvation and disease.

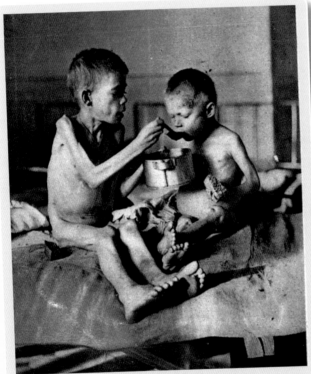

Children suffered particularly as a result of World War I. Many lived on the streets, and were without adequate food or clothing.

The Fight the Famine Council

People in England were not being told that this was happening in Germany and other European countries. A group of English women tried to tell the public about the suffering children by translating overseas news into English. They set up the Fight the **Famine** Council to publish and distribute information. They also campaigned to have enemy countries treated with justice and **compassion**. It was illegal to do this without government permission.

The blockade of Berlin in 1948 affected 2.5 million people. Despite airlifts of food by the Allied Forces, many of the young and sick died.

Glossary words

famine
a time when food is extremely scarce and people are starving

compassion
pity

"The Most Awful Spectacle in History."

MILLIONS OF CHILDREN NAKED AND STARVING IN EUROPE.

Every British Citizen Called Upon to Help— But it Must be To-day—To-morrow May Be Too Late.

WITH HUMAN DESTINY AT STAKE WILL YOU STAND IDLY BY?

Another Helpless Child is Dead—Another— and Another—While You Read—And Hesitate!

WE have won the War. We are justly proud. We are spending, on our well-earned amusements and our comfortable meals, millions of pounds every day!

And all the time, outside our very doors, a multitude of helpless children and stricken Mothers are perishing for want of food and clothes—not One Thousand, Two Thousand, or a Hundred Thousand, but MILLIONS! It is

2/- will Provide a Daily Dinner for One Child for One Week.
£1 will Feed and Clothe a Naked Starving Child.
£2 10s. will take an Ailing Child to Switzerland, where kindly Foster-Parents are ready to give it Three Months' Good Food and Nurse it Back to Health.
£100 will Feed 1,000 Children for One Week.

SUBSCRIPTIONS ON ACTIVE SERVICE WITHIN 24 HOURS

Whatever you can spare cannot be too small to be of value to the cause. Every penny you collect or subscribe will be immediately applied to the desperately urgent need of the starving and homeless. Within twenty-four hours your subscription will be doing active good, so perfect is the "Save the Children" Organisation—so eagerly helpful are its willing workers.

WHAT ONE PENNY WILL DO

The great call to our humanity and pity surely cannot fail to stir every generous feeling in our hearts. Nobody is asked to deny themselves. Pennies

Save the Children used newspaper publicity to get their message across.

More practical support

In 1919 the group had decided that just informing people was not enough. The children needed more practical support if they were going to survive. The Save the Children Fund was officially set up. Its purpose was to raise money to send to children in war-affected areas of Europe.

Successful publicity

The new organisation was very good at working with the media to get maximum publicity. It used newspaper advertisements and films to get its message across. Donations started to come in very quickly. One boy sent his pocket money. Another large cheque arrived pinned to one of the organisation's leaflets.

A permanent and effective body

The Save the Children Fund became very effective at providing food, clothing and money for children all over Europe. Although it was originally seen as a temporary organisation, it had to deal with a string of disasters in many different countries after the war ended. It dealt with these disasters so successfully that the Save the Children Fund eventually became a permanent body.

The founders of Save the Children

Dorothy Buxton and her sister Eglantyne Jebb were the main founders of Save the Children. They came from a well-educated family which was always concerned with the rights of others. Neither woman believed that war was ever a solution.

Informing the public

During World War I (1914–18), the sisters became concerned that the public was only hearing one side of what was happening in Europe. But by publishing information about the effect that the blockade was having on children, they were very soon in trouble. Eglantyne was arrested, tried and fined for handing out leaflets called 'A Starving Baby'.

Practical help

By 1919, the sisters decided that more practical help was needed. They formed the Fight the Famine Council, and later established the Save the Children Fund.

Ahead of their time

Dorothy was a strong and popular leader who could be very persuasive. She was committed to her work and had ideas about the welfare of children that were ahead of her time.

Eglantyne Jebb was passionate about the need to provide practical help for children who were affected by war.

Dorothy later lessened her involvement with Save the Children to concentrate on politics, and Eglantyne took her place. Eglantyne drafted the first Declaration of the Rights of the Child, with five main points, in 1923. The declaration was later adopted by the **United Nations**.

Glossary word

United Nations
an organisation made up of representatives from many countries, which deals with international peace and security

Did you know?

In 1919, Eglantyne Jebb was fined five pounds (which would be the same as a $4000 fine today) for handing out leaflets. She asked the lawyer who had argued the case against her in court for a donation!

Early work

During World War I, the British and their allies blockaded German-occupied cities like Berlin, in Germany, and Vienna, in Austria, to stop the transport of people and goods to these areas. This helped them to win the war, but caused great suffering to the civilian population. There were food shortages, which meant that many families had nothing to eat but cabbage and turnips.

Suffering children

This had severe effects, particularly on children, who were smaller and not as strong as the adults. There were reports that six-year-old children were so malnourished that they looked like two-year-olds. The lack of food made the children so weak that diseases such as **tuberculosis** and **rickets** spread rapidly. Children were dying in the street, wrapped in paper because they had no clothing. These conditions continued even after the fighting had stopped.

Raising money

At the beginning of 1919, Dorothy Buxton and her associates set up the Fight the Famine Council to campaign for justice and compassion for the defeated nations. They also began to raise money to send practical help to the children in Europe.

Glossary words

tuberculosis
an infectious disease where lumps form in parts of the body such as the lungs and bones, and cause those parts to break down

rickets
a bone weakness caused by a lack of vitamins

Dorothy Buxton formed the Fight the Famine Council, which was later to become the Save the Children Fund.

Core values of Save the Children

Core values are the things that a person, group or organisation really believes in. The values are used to work out rules of behaviour. The Save the Children Fund is an international group with many sub-branches in different countries around the world. The core values of the groups are sometimes expressed differently, but usually include:

Child-focus

Save the Children takes a child's view of the world and always works in the best interests of the child.

Independence

Save the Children is not influenced by any other group. Save the Children is prepared to speak out if necessary and take new approaches to help children.

Non-discrimination

Save the Children works without prejudice and does not take sides.

Participation

Save the Children believes in giving children the right to make their views known, and to be consulted and involved in decisions about their own futures.

Collaboration

Save the Children works with others whenever possible, in order to achieve more for children.

Accountability

Save the Children believes in being responsible to the children and communities it serves, and to its supporters. It reports honestly, has high standards and is efficient in its operation.

Did you know?

The families of 600 million children across the world have to survive on $1 each a day.

These children in Laos are reading books at a youth centre set up by Save the Children.

How Save the Children works

Once the immediate after effects of World War I began to ease, Save the Children was able to use donated funds for other situations. For example, through Save the Children, individuals could sponsor schoolhouses or help communities repair school buildings. They could provide students with meals, books and school supplies.

People could donate money for the needs of particular children and follow their progress. Although this can be beneficial, the problem with this approach is that a child or program can suddenly be left without support if the donor stops sending money.

Save the Children today

Today, Save the Children tries to work on a wider basis. It still aims to achieve lasting changes in children's rights, such as in health, education, disaster response and fighting abuse or **exploitation**. What is different today, is that people are not encouraged to donate for any one child or project. Individuals are still represented in media campaigns to raise funds, but are only representatives of an area in need. If many people donate money, the funds can be pooled for the greatest good. This means that the work can still continue, even if a few donors stop contributing.

Over half the Iraqi population is under the age of 14. The crisis for these children started long ago. For over ten years they have struggled to survive under UN sanctions imposed after the last Gulf War.

Save the Children has been supporting children and local communities in Iraq since 1991. With one of the largest presences in the region, we are determined to continue our vital work.

What Iraq's children urgently need now is your support. Please give all you can to help.

Iraq's forgotten casualties

Save the Children

The International Save the Children Alliance is the world's leading independent children's rights and development organisation, with national offices in 29 countries and operational programs in over 100.

Donations can be made on-line at:
www.savethechildren.org.au or
by mail to Iraq Emergency Appeal, Save the Children Australia, PO Box 767, Hawthorn VIC 3122.
ABN 99 008 610 035

Please accept my gift of:_____ ☐ I enclose my cheque (payable to Save the Children Australia)
Or charge my: ☐ Bankcard ☐ MasterCard ☐ Visa ☐ AMEX

Cardholder's name:_____
Signature_____ Card Expiry Date __/__ AMEX ID#_____
Name (Title First Surname)_____ Telephone_____
Address_____ Postcode_____
Any information given to Save the Children Australia is protected by our Privacy Policy
GIFTS OF $2 AND OVER ARE TAX DEDUCTIBLE

Save the Children uses images of children to help raise awareness about particular areas that are in need of help.

Where in the world is Save the Children?

Save the Children works in many countries around the world. This map shows where some major Save the Children campaigns are located.

North

Arctic Ocean

North and Central America

Europe

Asia and the Middle East

Atlantic Ocean

Tropic of Cancer

Pacific Ocean

Africa

Equator

Pacific Ocean

South America

Indian Ocean

Tropic of Capricorn

Pacific Reg

Southern Ocean

Timeline

Save the Children has been working to help people since it began in 1919.

1919	Save the Children Fund is founded by Dorothy Buxton and Eglantyne Jebb.
1920s	Eglantyne Jebb writes the first Declaration of the Rights of the Child.
1930s	Save the Children extends its work from Europe into Africa. Dorothy Buxton pleads with the Nazis to respect children's rights in World War II (1939–45).
1940s	Displaced children are rescued in Europe after the war. Save the Children begins working in India.
1950s	Save the Children works with 100 000 homeless children who are suffering from diseases and malnutrition after the Korean War.
1959	Eglantyne Jebb's Declaration on the Rights of the Child is adopted by the United Nations.
1960s	Save the Children launches its first 'Freedom from Hunger' campaign.
1970s	Save the Children begins emergency work in Africa and Central America. Stop Polio campaign is launched.
1980s	Save the Children works to help victims of famine in Africa. Save the Children does its first work on HIV/AIDS (a virus that stops the body from fighting against infections) campaigns.
1988	The International Save the Children Alliance is created.
1990s	Save the Children begins working on the human rights of child soldiers and displaced children after wars.
2002	Save the Children members use the same logo.
2003	Save the Children responds to the outbreak of conflict in Iraq, delivering aid to schools, orphanages and hospitals, as well as transporting children to schools, raising awareness about the dangers of unexploded bombs and mines, and working to prevent abductions.
2004	Save the Children publishes its 'State of the World's Mothers' report. Save the Children distributes plastic sheeting for shelter, jerry cans for retrieving and storing water, and thousands of blankets, while also distributing food to more than 100 000 internally displaced people in Sudan.

y to countries

ACIFIC REGION
ustralia, Fiji,
ew Zealand,
pua New Guinea,
lomon Islands,
nuatu

SIA AND THE IDDLE EAST
ghanistan, Azerbaijan,
menia, Bangladesh,
utan, Burma
Myanmar), Cambodia,
ina, Hong Kong,
dia, Indonesia, Iran,
aq, Japan, Jordan,
rgyzstan, Laos,
banon, Mongolia,
rth Korea, Nepal,
akistan, Philippines,
uth Korea, Sri Lanka,
jikistan, Thailand,
zbekistan, Vietnam,
ongolia, West Bank/
aza, Yemen

UROPE
bania,
osnia–Herzegovina,
ulgaria, Croatia,
enmark, Estonia,
nland, Georgia,
reenland, Iceland,
osovo, Lithuania,
acedonia, Moldova,
etherlands, Norway,
omania, Russian
ederation, Serbia,
pain, Sweden,
nited Kingdom

AFRICA
Angola, Burkina Faso,
Burundi, Egypt, Eritrea,
Ethiopia, Ghana,
Guinea, Guinea Bissau,
Côte d'Ivoire, Lesotho,
Liberia, Malawi, Mali,
Morocco, Mozambique,
Nigeria, Rwanda,
Senegal, Sierra Leone,
South Africa, Sudan,
Swaziland, Zambia,
Zimbabwe

NORTH AND CENTRAL AMERICA
Canada, Cuba,
Dominican Republic,
El Salvador, Guatemala,
Haiti, Honduras, Mexico,
Nicaragua, United
States of America

SOUTH AMERICA
Bolivia, Brazil, Colombia,
Peru, Argentina, Chile,
Ecuador, Paraguay,
El Salvador, Venezuela

Concerns, campaigns and classic actions

Save the Children is concerned about a range of problems throughout the world. It identifies specific campaigns and takes action accordingly.

CONCERNS

Inadequate health care

Save the Children is concerned that millions of children die every year from diseases that can be prevented or easily treated. Many others suffer from poor health throughout their childhood and cannot reach their full potential.

CAMPAIGNS

Save the Children runs programs throughout the world to improve the health of mothers and children. The basic cause of much illness, particularly in **developing countries**, is poverty. Poverty leads to people living in unhealthy conditions, and prevents them eating healthy diets or getting medical care when they need it.

Save the Children works with all sorts of government and non-government groups to provide good quality, cheap health care wherever it is needed. Even countries that appear to be well off can have areas where children are not getting proper medical services. Save the Children can train health workers, supply equipment and provide buildings to make a difference in these children's lives.

By improving the health of pregnant women, Save the Children can help to improve the health of children before they are even born. Eight million babies each year are either stillborn or die before they are one month old. Expectant mothers need immunisation against diseases and extra nutrition. They need skilled attendants at the birth. They need to be educated about danger signs during and after their pregnancy, and they need access to information about the best care for their child.

This mother and child in Mozambique received care from the Mobile Health Brigade, a project supported by Save the Children.

Glossary words

developing countries
countries that are not yet able to provide a good standard of living for their citizens in such areas as health, education and housing

As many as 30 000 children die every day from diseases that can be easily prevented or treated. The worst of these are measles, **tetanus** in babies, pneumonia, diarrhoea and **malaria**. Simple measures such as immunisation, extra nutrients like Vitamin A and basic treatment to replace fluids can save thousands of lives. Save the Children works with local partners to provide this care in over 100 countries. They also run programs on breastfeeding and HIV/AIDS prevention and care.

HIV/AIDS has killed more than 20 million people worldwide. It still threatens the health of tens of millions of children in developing countries, particularly in Africa. It has affected many communities so badly that they are losing any progress in health, education and business that had previously been made. Save the Children works to prevent new HIV infections, especially among young and high-risk groups, and helps individual communities to provide care and support for the children and families affected.

Classic action

Save the Children has worked to rebuild many schools in Iraq.

Save the Children is operating a large program in Iraq after the 2003 war. A health, safety and landmine awareness project has been delivered to 15 000 children and adults. Clean water and **sanitation** systems have been supplied, as well as medical supplies for mothers and babies. Schools and clinics that were destroyed during the fighting have been rebuilt.

Glossary words

tetanus
a disease that causes dangerous muscle spasms

malaria
a fever spread by mosquitoes

sanitation
drainage and disposal of sewage

Inadequate education

Save the Children is concerned that many children in the world do not have access to a reasonable standard of education. There are strong connections between a lack of education, poverty and poor health.

CAMPAIGNS

Around the world, 125 million children are not in school. Two-thirds of these are girls. Improved access to education, particularly for girls, is urgently needed. Girls will often grow up to raise families, and education will help them to do a much better job. This also has effects on the wider community. Save the Children is involved in providing education programs for people of all ages around the world.

When Save the Children operates an education program, it always uses the following approaches:

- The local communities are involved. Any project with local support draws more people in, brings something to the entire community and works against poverty. It is also much more likely to continue.

- All learning is centred around the children and takes place in ways that are acceptable to the community. Local languages and customs are followed.

- Everyone shares in the costs of building and running schools. Costs are kept as low as possible.

- Programs are monitored to find the best ways of helping children to learn.

Save the Children improves the education of girls in many developing countries around the world.

As well as working with young children, Save the Children helps develop programs for older youths and adults as well. Youth development programs might be based around personal growth, or be connected to learning a trade. These programs can also be a part of the peace process in countries that have been affected by conflict. Learning to solve problems by **negotiation** and the use of **arbitrators** is the focus of these programs.

Programs for adults are often about reading and writing. In many countries, people have had no opportunity to learn these skills. This could have been because of a lack of schools, wars or poverty. They cannot get good jobs, and can be cheated in business. Parents who are literate often use better child rearing methods and encourage their children to go to school. If people can read and write, then the whole community benefits.

Many women in Bangladesh, who would not otherwise have had access to education, are learning to read and write as a result of literacy classes run the Save the Children.

Classic action

In Bangladesh, T… worked as a servant because her family did not have enough money to send her to school. She married early and had two children. After her husband died, T… attended a Save the Children group and learned how to read. Soon, T… was able to understand signs in her village and doctor's prescriptions. She could also help her daughter with her school work. Now T… runs her own business.

Glossary words

negotiation
a discussion held to reach an agreement or compromise

arbitrators
people appointed to settle a dispute

Lack of children's rights

Save the Children is concerned about the lack of children's rights in many countries throughout the world. The United Nations has agreed on a set of rights that all children should be entitled to. Many children still do not get these rights and are in urgent need of protection.

CAMPAIGNS

In 1923, Eglantyne Jebb wrote the first Declaration of the Rights of the Child, which later became the United Nations Convention on the Rights of the Child. The Convention recognised that a special set of rights was needed for children, because they could not always fight for themselves. The Convention stated that all children had the right to:

- equal treatment
- receive food and shelter
- receive health care and education
- protection from violence, abuse and neglect
- protection from such things as performing adult work or being used as soldiers.

Save the Children bases all its work on its support for the Rights of the Child. They particularly care for groups such as refugees and street children, who are often heavily discriminated against. Girls and sufferers of HIV/AIDS are two other groups in need of special protection. Save the Children works to challenge discrimination, help children understand their rights, and put pressure on governments and other players to respect the rights of all children.

Save the Children first began helping street children during World War I. Today it is trying to provide help to children all over the world, including Cambodia.

Save the Children encourages children to take part in their society. It funds citizenship education and has, on various occasions, arranged for children to take part in important conferences such as those run by the United Nations.

Save the Children also runs programs to help disabled children take an active part in their own families and communities, so that they are not discriminated against or sent to institutions.

In some countries, girls are treated very differently to boys. Girls may be given less food, less education or treated as servants. Save the Children investigates the reasons for these differences and develops education programs to encourage change.

Many children, particularly refugees, also suffer from racism. This can affect them from a very early age. They may be discriminated against because of their culture, language or religion. Save the Children runs programs to support these children, and to educate others so that they may be treated more fairly.

Classic action

In the United Kingdom, the Scotland Training Program educates the community about children's rights. It has developed a Toolkit, or set of suggestions, to encourage young people to have a say in the services, groups and rules that affect their lives.

This training centre in England offers childcare and training for childcare workers.

Lack of emergency protection

Save the Children is concerned that, in times of emergencies and disasters, such as wars, famines or earthquakes, children are at particular risk. Children are physically weaker than adults, and may become separated from their families who generally care for them. In these situations they are in much greater danger of harm or exploitation.

CAMPAIGNS

Save the Children began as a response to the effects of World War I. Today it is still providing basic necessities for those affected by emergencies, but it now also works towards long-term recovery and **redevelopment**. Some emergencies happen without much warning, but others can be predicted. Save the Children investigates ways to prevent disasters if possible, and sets up plans to lessen their effects in the future.

In attempting to help prevent famine, Save the Children has set up a survey that can be used by governments to take action. For example, a government may be able to prevent starvation by importing supplies from other areas or countries.

Save the Children also helps to build systems to provide clean water supplies. It can send experts to developing countries to teach people better ways of growing crops, by using irrigation and taking care of the soil. It can supply seeds, tools and fishing gear so that families can feed themselves. It can also advise people on how to care for their animals.

By building systems to provide clean water, Save the Children is helping whole communities. This pond was built in Ethiopia.

Glossary word

redevelopment
rebuilding the structures of a country, such as health and education systems, transport and food production

Children who have been affected by wars have three main needs:
- material things such as food, shelter and clothes
- protection from any more physical or mental harm, and help to cope with the harm they have already suffered
- access to education and time for play, to allow them to develop into balanced adults.

During times of conflict, it is easy for children to be exploited by adults who use them as soldiers, adult workers or for sex. Save the Children tries to keep families together and to reunite lost children with their parents. In situations where this is not possible, it tries to find substitute carers. Save the Children campaigns around the world for more money to be spent on the care and protection of children in these sorts of situations. It also tries to prevent children from being exploited during peacetime, when they may be forced to work in places like factories.

Classic action

Afghanistan has suffered from 20 years of war as well as the effects of a terrible drought. Save the Children is struggling to help 300 000 people get enough food and adequate health care. Children, particularly, are in danger from fighting and crime, which is still going on. Save the Children is attempting to protect these children and to provide some basic education for them.

Save the Children provides health eduction classes such as this one in Afghanistan.

The people of Save the Children

Save the Children helps people and communities all over the world. Here are four people who use their own specialised skills to help in different situations.

WORKNESH MEKONNEN — Director of fundraising and sponsorship

Worknesh Mekonnen is determined to help Save the Children build more schools for the many children who are still missing out on basic education in Ethiopia.

Since 1997, Worknesh Mekonnen has worked for Save the Children in Ethiopia, Africa. She chose this organisation because of her strong desire to be a part of the process of improving the lives of **disadvantaged** children and their communities. In Ethiopia today, many young people are unemployed, and their numbers are increasing. Worknesh would like them to live in a more hopeful environment. She hopes that her work will create opportunities for them to have more productive and meaningful lives.

In September 2000, Worknesh became the leader of a new education project in the western part of Ethiopia. This gave her the chance to take some direct action to help her country's children. As a part of this project, she was able to open three new community-based schools in three remote villages. The numbers of people who came to enrol overwhelmed her. This made Worknesh even more determined to build other schools and bring education to hundreds of children who were still missing out. In less than two years since the first three schools were opened, Save the Children has built nine more community-based schools.

Glossary word

disadvantaged
having a difficulty in some area, such as health, income or education, which prevents the person from leading a full life

Did you know?

Ethiopia cannot afford to provide fully trained teachers for its schools. Save the Children finds Ethiopians with 10–12 years of education and a little teacher training, and helps them to teach basic reading, writing and arithmetic to children.

This is a community school in Ethiopia.

Worknesh finds her work with Save the Children extremely satisfying. She says there is nothing more exciting than seeing children going to school, enjoying clean drinking water and having access to health facilities. All of these things, which are taken for granted in wealthy countries, will allow these children to have a better future.

Not everyone Worknesh meets is as committed as she is. She sometimes finds it frustrating and upsetting to deal with people who do not share her vision for a better life for Ethiopian youth. Worknesh copes with this by planning different ways to get the work done without them, or ways to change their minds!

The kind of job that Worknesh does is not easy. She spends long days working with the people in different communities, followed by many hours in the office. This means she is sometimes not able to spend as much time with her own family as she would like. She tries to find some kind of balance between the different parts of her life, and to involve her family in her work when she can. They understand the importance of what she does, and the great efforts needed to bring about real change in their country to provide a better future for everyone.

Did you know?

Seventy six per cent of Ethiopians do not have access to improved water supplies.

GARY SHAYE Field office director

Gary Shaye gets a tremendous degree of satisfaction from his work with Save the Children.

Gary Shaye has been with Save the Children since 1974, and is currently the field office director for the program in Bolivia. As a young man he was a volunteer with the Peace Corps, a United States overseas volunteer service especially for young people. After that experience, he decided that he wanted a career in international development. He went back to university for extra qualifications and has worked for Save the Children ever since. He likes the way the organisation works directly with communities, as this assists Save the Children to learn about national policy changes that will make the greatest difference.

One of Gary's most interesting jobs was starting a program in Nepal. Nepal is a tiny country to the north of India. Both Nepal and its neighbour, Bhutan, were in great need of better health and education services. Gary helped to establish these programs by working closely with the local governments. In Bhutan, he trained and advised students who had studied outside the country, and travelled through remote parts of Bhutan to visit them when they were on community service assignments. Gary later returned to field work in Bolivia.

Did you know?

Only 38 out of every 100 Bolivian children complete school to grade-8 level.

In Bolivia, Gary is particularly proud of a special program for teenagers called 'Making Decisions'. The program assists young people in thinking about the future, and helps them to consider which careers might be right for them. The program also gives information about health issues. It has been very successful in helping teenagers avoid unwanted pregnancies. Gary would like to see this program expand to other parts of the country. He would also like to assist other aid organisations adapt this work to their own programs.

Gary has worked at various levels of the organisation, and previously served as the Vice President for International Programs. This gave him a good chance to see what Save the Children was doing all over the world. He has seen the programs really make a difference at an individual level, such as saving the lives of babies and providing children with a quality education.

Gary's family has also seen places that ordinary travellers never see, and they have had the opportunity to learn other languages and experience new cultures. Together they have travelled to Africa and the Middle East, as well as to Bolivia and Bhutan. At times, Gary has a lot of responsibilities and his family has to sacrifice some of their time with him. But at the same time, being able to travel with him has given them many unique and wonderful memories. They all agree that the positives outweigh the negatives.

Gary is working with this teenage girl as part of a contraceptives workshop for adolescents in Bolivia.

FIONA FARLEY Project manager, education

Fiona Farley gets a great deal of enjoyment from her work with Save the Children.

Fiona Farley started work with Save the Children four years ago as the project manager for a basic education and teacher training project in Vietnam. Before this, she had helped to train teachers in Papua New Guinea, and she wanted to continue this work in Asia.

Fiona's work with Save the Children involves showing teachers better ways to teach their classes. She also helps to develop new resources for them to use in classrooms. She is involved in the renovation of school buildings and the provision of better equipment for the children.

Fiona has travelled to remote areas, through flooded rivers, and has eaten some very unusual lunches, such as sea snails and boiled porcupine.

The best part of Fiona's job is seeing the changes that the Save the Children program has made in schools. Where children once sat perfectly still and were afraid to speak, they are now enjoying new learning games and teaching aids which make their lessons fun. Their teachers have learned new methods of managing their classes, and education is a much happier process for everyone.

Did you know?

The Basic Education and Teacher Training program in Vietnam operates in 40 schools and benefits 20 000 children.

By helping to train even a few teachers, Save the Children can improve the education of many children in Vietnam.

The project workers have also spent a lot of time writing and illustrating children's books for their schools. The children in Vietnamese schools have a very limited choice of books and many only ever experience reading from a textbook. Storybooks and big books written just for the enjoyment of reading are very rare in Vietnam. Fiona hopes that the books they are writing will be published, and that more can be produced.

This Save the Children project is only funded for a limited period, but Fiona hopes that more money will be found to allow it to continue. The project has already attracted a lot of attention. Visitors have come from all over Vietnam to see the teaching materials and resources that are being developed, and to learn new teaching skills.

Fiona would like to continue her work in Vietnam, even though it can be challenging. When her father died in Australia, she felt very cut off from her family, even though she was able to return briefly for his funeral. Her Vietnamese friends and their culture were a great comfort then, and her work gives her so much enjoyment that she couldn't bear to think about stopping.

Did you know?

When a person dies in Vietnam, a special ancestral altar is set up with a photograph, candles, incense and prayer beads. Flowers and fruit are placed there every day for a year.

ADAM KEEHN Field office director

Adam Keehn works for Save the Children in Ethiopia.

Adam Keehn began his humanitarian work with the Peace Corps, a United States overseas volunteer service, in Africa in 1982. After three years he returned to America, married, then moved back to Africa in 1986. He later returned to America for further study in international development to make him better equipped for the work he had come to love, before returning to Africa once more.

Now he works in Ethiopia in one of the most memorable programs of his experience. Adam's job is to deliver food aid to the millions of Ethiopians who need help. Save the Children has set up a series of Therapeutic Feeding Centres across the country, which save the lives of children who will die if they are not given urgent treatment. First, the centres provide medical examinations, **vaccinations** and vitamin supplements. After this, children are put on a program of feeding with enriched milk, which restores their health after only a few weeks. When the children are ready to return to their villages, they are given extra food and clothing to keep them going. Staff from Save the Children make follow-up visits to check their progress.

Did you know?

More than 50 per cent of Ethiopian children under the age of five are considered stunted because of poor nutrition.

Glossary words
vaccinations
medicines given to protect against infectious diseases

Adam often has very mixed feelings about his work. While he loves what he does and is proud of the work, the suffering of the local people distresses him. He sees children begging on the streets, becoming ill from lack of fresh water, food or proper shelter. It is also hard for his own young children to understand how things can be so different for them. They are not rich by American standards, but are extremely wealthy compared to most Ethiopians.

At the same time, Adam feels satisfaction at what Save the Children has been able to do. Some parents walk for days to bring their dying children to a feeding centre. It is a joy to see these same children return home later, healthy and with support for the future. In some areas, for example, Save the Children is teaching women to make yoghurt and butter to help support their families. Communities are digging huge ponds to store water for their animals during the long dry season.

Adam hopes that Save the Children will be able to join with other organisations to provide even better help in the future. He also hopes that it will be able to convince wealthy countries that they need to do much more to help developing countries.

Did you know?

During 2003, 26 feeding centres saved the lives of thousands of Ethiopian children.

These women and children are at a Save the Children feeding centre in Ethiopia.

What can you do?

There are many ways in which you can help Save the Children in their work.

Child Link project

Some groups of young people support Save the Children by joining the Child Link project. As part of the Child Link project, you can choose a community from somewhere in the world that needs support. The group regularly sends money which is used to build better health, education or business opportunities. A child from the community is chosen as a representative so that the group can have a personal connection.

Fundraising activities

Many local Save the Children groups also organise fundraising activities. Fashion shows, quiz nights and concerts have all been held to collect money. Volunteers also do direct collections at shopping centres.

Spreading information

Young people can also be involved in spreading information about Save the Children activities. Many national branches of the organisation can provide magazines or speakers.

Shopping

Even shopping can help. In some countries, and via the Internet, there are Save the Children shops. Products sold in these shops help provide money to keep the work going.

Save the Children publishes a magazine called World's Children *to help inform people about the organisation's ongoing work.*

Glossary

arbitrators	people appointed to settle a dispute
compassion	pity
developing countries	countries that are not yet able to provide a good standard of living for their citizens in such areas as health, education and housing
disadvantaged	having a difficulty in some area, such as health, income or education, which prevents the person from leading a full life
exploitation	using someone, or something, in a harmful way for your own benefit
famine	a time when food is extremely scarce and people are starving
human rights	a set of rights, such as the right to a fair trial, laid down by the United Nations
humanitarian	devoted to people's welfare and the promotion of social reform
malaria	a fever spread by mosquitoes
negotiation	a discussion held to reach an agreement or compromise
redevelopment	rebuilding the structures of a country, such as health and education systems, transport and food production
rickets	a bone weakness caused by a lack of vitamins
sanitation	drainage and disposal of sewage
tetanus	a disease that causes dangerous muscle spasms
tuberculosis	an infectious disease where lumps form in parts of the body such as the lungs and bones, and cause those parts to break down
United Nations	an organisation made up of representatives from many countries, which deals with international peace and security
United Nations convention	a treaty or legal agreement, for example, about children's rights, signed by the member countries of the UN
vaccinations	medicines given to protect against infectious diseases
volunteers	people who donate their time to a cause

Index

B

babies 14–15, 25
Buxton, Dorothy 8, 9, 13

C

child exploitation 11, 18, 20–21
child labour 18, 21
child rights 5, 8, 13, 18–19
child soldiers 13, 18, 21
community development 5, 11, 14–15, 19, 20, 24–5, 26–7, 29
core values 10

D

disaster response 11, 13, 20–21
donations 4, 7, 9, 11, 22, 30

E

education 11, 13, 14, 16–17, 19, 21, 22–7,
ethics 10

F

famine 6, 7, 9, 13, 20–21
feeding centres 28–9

G

girls 16–17, 18, 19

H

health 11, 13, 14–15, 16, 24–5, 28–9
history 6–9, 13
HIV/AIDS 13, 15, 18
homeless children 13, 18

I

independence 10

J

Jebb, Eglantyne 8, 13, 18

L

landmines 13, 15
literacy 16–17
locations 12–13

M

malnutrition 9, 13, 28–9
mothers 13, 14–15, 17

N

neutrality 10

P

poverty, effects of 14, 16
prevention of disasters 20
publicity 6, 7, 8, 11, 30

R

redevelopment 20, 24–5, 29
refugees 13, 18, 19

S

sanitation 15

T

teacher training 22, 26–7

U

United Nations Convention on the Rights of the Child 5, 8, 13, 18

V

vaccination 14–15
volunteers 22–9, 30

W

war 6, 8, 9, 11, 13, 20–21
water 15, 20, 29
World War I 6–7, 8, 9, 20

Y

youth development 17, 25